YOUR KNOWLEDGE HAS VALUE

Bibliographic information published by the German National Library:

The German National Library lists this publication in the National Bibliography;
detailed bibliographic data are available on the Internet at http://dnb.dnb.de .

Imprint:

Copyright © 2008 GRIN Verlag, Open Publishing GmbH
Print and binding: Books on Demand GmbH, Norderstedt Germany
ISBN: 9783656515975

This book at GRIN:

http://www.grin.com/en/e-book/151090/discussion-essay-on-the-short-story-soldier-
s-home-by-ernest-hemingway

Katharina Ochsenfahrt

Discussion essay on the short story "Soldier's Home" by Ernest Hemingway

How does Krebs's mother embody the community's values and what does Krebs think of those values?

GRIN Publishing

GRIN - Your knowledge has value

Since its foundation in 1998, GRIN has specialized in publishing academic texts by students, college teachers and other academics as e-book and printed book. The website www.grin.com is an ideal platform for presenting term papers, final papers, scientific essays, dissertations and specialist books.

Visit us on the internet:

http://www.grin.com/

http://www.facebook.com/grincom

http://www.twitter.com/grin_com

Name: Katharina Ochsenfahrt   Semester: 2

Class: Academic Writing I, Mon.14.15-15.45   Date:17.07.2008

How does Krebs's mother embody the community's values and what does Krebs think of those values?

Discussion essay on the short story "Soldier's Home" by Ernest Hemingway

Relationships between parents and their children are never easy, because they belong to different generation, and have therefore different values in life. This often leads to conflicts. But in the short story *Soldier's Home* by Ernest Hemingway the protangonist Krebs and his mother do not have an usual generation conflict. Krebs has a changed character, because he has been to war. He does not have an aim in his life anymore. Krebs's mother embodies the community's values, and she makes Krebs start an adult life against his will. *This includes that she encourages him to find a job, and a girlfriend. Moreover, she wants him to believe in God, and to show affection for her and the rest of the family.*

Krebs's mother wants Krebs to find a job. At the beginning of the story Krebs has no aim in his life. He lives everyday in the same pattern, and he does not want to change anything

1

about that. He did not even think about finding a job. But Krebs's mother wants her son to develope, to forget the war, and to start an own, independent life. She tells him that everyone has to work. This is the first community value, which is embodied by her. Moreover, she talks about a young man, who is about Krebs's age and has a good job. She wants to convince him to go, and find an occupation, so that he can start an autonomous life.

She encourages him to take some girls out, and to find a girlfriend. Before she talks to him he does not seem to have a great interest in girls. Actually he would have liked to have a girlfriend, but he did not want to work for it. This is because he was not able to maintain a relationship to anyone, because of his lack to show feelings. Then Krebs' prents allow him to use the father's car. They permit this, because they think he will leave the house more often, become autonomous, and maybe find a girlfriend. Moreover, Krebs's mother tells him that this young man, who was already mentioned, is going to be married. She obviously wants Krebs to get married, too. This shows that she embodies the value that young men should marry.

She talks about the will of God, and she wants Krebs to pray with her. God plays an important roll in Krebs's family. It is said that Krebs has been to a religious college before he went to war. After he returned he has lost his believe, because of his experiences. When his mother asks him:" Would you kneel and pray with me, Harold?" (Hemingway 127), he answers "I can't."(127) After that Krebs's mother tries to make him pray, because she thinks that the community expects the people to be religious, but he does not want to. So she prays for him to compensate his lack of believe in God.

Krebs's mother wants her son to show feelings for his familiy. After Krebs returned from war, he was not able to speak about his experiences, and later he felt that no one would listen to it, so he did not tell anyone about his feelings. Sometimes he even told lies. He imagined extraorinary stories to catch people's attention. But most of the time he did not talk about anything. He does not seem to have a relationship to anybody. But his mother tries to get contact to him, to talk to him, and to influence him. When she finally asks him:"Don't you love your mother dear boy?"(126), he answers "no"(126). He even adds: "I don't love anybody" (126). This shows his unablility to have relationships and the show emotions. His mother is very shocked about his answer and starts crying. This indicates that she embodies the value, that childen must love their parents. By her crying she somehow force Krebs to show feeling, and to apologize. After that he even wants to go to his sisters baseball game. His attitude has change. He now tries to care for other people and to maintain relationships. In this way his mother made him show affection for his familiy.

To sum up, Krebs's mother influences him so much, that at the end of the short story he decides to go to Kansas City, and find a job there. He only does this to make her happy, not because he wants it. Moreover, this shory shows what a huge impact parents have on their children. Usually children would do nearly everything to make their parents proud. By taking the advice of his mother, Krebs started a new life. He will become a young man, who is respected by the community, and his mother will be very satisfied.

(words: 934)

Work Cited:

Hemingway, Ernest. "Soldier's Home." *The Short Stories of Ernest Hemingway.* Reader Academic Writing I. http://www.cis.vt.edu/modernworld/d/hemingway.html#3

YOUR KNOWLEDGE HAS VALUE

- We will publish your bachelor's and master's thesis, essays and papers

- Your own eBook and book - sold worldwide in all relevant shops

- Earn money with each sale

Upload your text at www.GRIN.com and publish for free